# TRUMP POEMS

It is better to keep your mouth closed and let
people think you are a fool than to open it and
remove all doubt.

*. . . . . . Mark Twain*


The truth is incontrovertible. Malice may attack
it, ignorance may deride it, but in the end, there
it is.

*. . . . . . Winston Churchill*

Other books by Tom Greening:

*Animals I Have Known*
*Fruits & Veggies I Have Known*
*Holocaust Poems: A Gentile's Perspective*
*Instant  Relief: Encyclopedia of Self-Help*
*Jazz Poems*
*Nasreddin the Psychologist*
*Poems For and About Elders*
*Poems for Yale Classmates*
*Tolstoy's Lament*
*War Poems: Reflections by a Fortunate American*
*Words Against the Void*

# TRUMP

poems

by Tom Greening

GARDEN WALL PUBLISHERS

GARDEN WALL
PUBLISHERS

Garden Wall Publishers
Sherman Oaks, California
www.gardenwallpublishers.com
kenmozo@kenrmac.com

**TRUMP POEMS**



Tom Greening
3923 Benedict Canyon
Sherman Oaks, CA 91423
tgreening@saybrook.edu
818-784-2895
818-681-1661 cell
www.tomgreening.com

Designed by Ken Rubin

Available at Amazon.com
Paperback and Kindle

**ISBN**: 9781796473490

If you look at any successful professional - a salesperson, a marketer, a real estate agent, a trader - they all have the same qualities as the con man. The only difference is that one side uses their talents in the right direction and the con man is taking the easy way out.

. . . . . . . . *Frank Abagnale*

# Table of Contents

TRUMP
MAKE
AMERICA
GREAT AGAIN!

# DONALD WILL FLAME OUT

I fear you'll think I'm arrogant and vain,
but I must brag: Today I did refrain
from glancing even once at the TV,
thus kept Herr Trump from aggravating me.
A day of bliss, pretending life is good
and leaders of our land act like they should.
This farce shall pass, and Donald will flame out.
Let's hope that's soon and sure without a doubt.
We will survive, as Rome did for a while.
Perhaps we'll find a leader far less vile.

# IMPEACH THIS LOON

Come back, MacDuff, our nation looks to you–
From ancient times we now must take our cue.
How did those trees proceed to Dunsinane?
The time has come for them to march again.
A narcissistic despot must not rule.
Our fate is greatly menaced by this fool.
Where is the knight who forthwith will depose
this emperor who clearly has no clothes?
To save our nation from a tragic fate.
impeach this loon before it is too late.

# MY LIE ABOUT TRUMP

I used to claim, "I cannot tell a lie,"
but now that time has very long gone by.
I tell a hundred of them every week,
at least a few each time I deign to speak.
Reality has lost its grasp on me–
Prevarication–that's my specialty.
In politics I've found a worthy theme,
and hope I can recruit you to my team.
I'll swear to you that up is really down,
that Trump is really not a toxic clown.
Reality has lost its grasp on me–
Prevarication–that's my specialty.
In politics I've found a worthy theme,
and hope I can recruit you to my team.
I'll swear to you that up is really down,
that Trump is really not a toxic clown.

# SAVE OURSELVES FROM TRUMP?

I hope we notice very soon
that Trump's a menacing buffoon,
a clown, a dolt, but dangerous,
to reasoning impervious.
Led by a boor with feet of clay,
our nation's peril grows each day.
Can he be stopped, can wisdom reign,
or will Rome's fall transpire again?
How can we throw The Donald out
and save ourselves from this crude lout?

# TRUMP THE MUTANT MIME

The circus has turned loose its clown
who soon will bring our nation down.
Our country once prized saner men,
but this is now and that was then.
I'm sadly grieving all the time—
we're governed by a mutant mime.
There was a time when, foolishly,
I thought I could serve usefully,
but now I have abandoned hope—
We're sliding down a slippery slope.
We have eschewed sobriety
and follow Trump toward tragedy.

# TRUMP REGARDS HIS JOB

This job is harder than I thought it'd be,
requiring thought and some maturity.
I figured it would be a fancy show
without demanding skills I'd need to know.
I like the pomp, but not the complex work,
which threatens to expose me as a jerk.
That fellow Kim keeps aggravating me
and should be fired peremptorily.
I'll strut and rant in presidential style
and then move on in just a little while.

# SURVIVING TRUMP

No pill exists to quell this angst of mine.
No God has vowed to give me a clear sign
that I am saved or maybe just let go,
but still my wiener dog adores me, so
I scold and trim my errant climbing vine,
assure my friends that I am feeling fine,
ignore the Trumpian madness on TV,
pray that somewhere there still is sanity.
Our nation has survived gross fools before.
Let's shove this yahoo out the nearest door.

# SURVIVE THE CON

I'm stumbling in the dark, bereft and dazed.
I steadily grow desperate and crazed.
The world is cracking up, or is it I?
Is each bright truth a convoluted lie?
A con man now can game the government–
to flagrant lies he's built a monument.
I'm told that down is up and up is down,
I'm urged to trust a psychopathic clown.
Yes, winter's come, and spring is lost at sea.
Survive 'til summer?  We must wait and see.

# TRUMP'S FALL

We soon will see doomed Donald fall-
this fool who makes no sense at all.
Where is our bard, our Sophocles,
to chart the course of his disease?
Could Chaucer, Shakespeare, Milton, Pope
begin to show the tragic scope
of what unfolds on our TV,
this threat to our fraught destiny?
The Furies hover, smirk with glee,
while we're engulfed by tragedy.

# WE MUST IMPEACH

By now it's become evident
we've got a loony president.
Let's help our nation Trump survive
and keep democracy alive.
Which patriot will make the speech
to start the process to impeach
this idiot and then resume
our efforts to prevent our doom?
His madness grows, the time is nigh–
don't let our blessed nation die!

# TRUMP PERIL

I am a patriotic frump
who's horrified by Donald Trump.
We're all in peril while he rules,
this grandiose foremost of fools.
How can we make him go away
or keep this rabid dog at bay?
Quick– fetch a net and capture him
before he launches on some whim.
Though he will howl, pontificate,
we must avoid a tragic fate.

# TRUMPIAN POMPOSITY

Of my old stalwart company
who now retains grit, dignity?
My heroes, once so fit and hale,
have staggered off to some dark vale,
and in their place what do we see?
Crass Trumpian pomposity.
This poem's an arrow I'll let fly
into the vast and stolid sky.
Will someone read it and then be
redeemer of our destiny?

9 781796 473490